MERINA

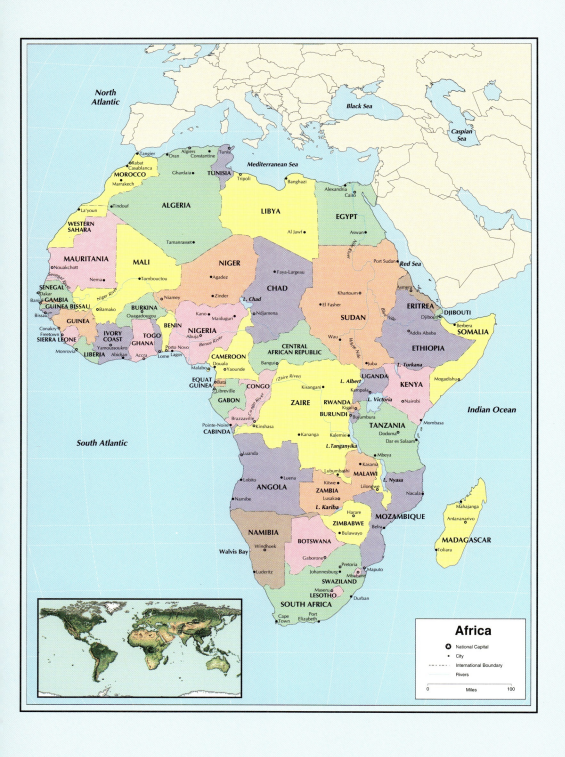

The Heritage Library of African Peoples

MERINA

Rebecca L. Green, Ph.D.

THE ROSEN PUBLISHING GROUP, INC.
NEW YORK

Published in 1997 by The Rosen Publishing Group, Inc.
29 East 21st Street, New York, NY 10010

Copyright 1997 by The Rosen Publishing Group, Inc.

All rights reserved. No part of this book may be reproduced in any form without permission in writing from the publisher, except by a reviewer.

First Edition

Manufactured in the United States of America

Library of Congress Cataloging-in-Publication Data

Green, Rebecca L.
  Merina / Rebecca L. Green. — 1st ed.
    p.   cm. — (The Heritage library of African peoples)
  Includes bibliographical references and index.
  Summary: Describes the culture, history, and contemporary life of the Merina people of Madagascar.
  ISBN 0-8239-1991-9
  1. Merina (Malagasy people)—Juvenile literature.   [1. Merina (Malagasy people)]   I. Title.   II. Series.
DT469.M277M4745   1996
969.1—dc20   96-22944
                                                            CIP
                                                             AC

Contents

	Introduction	6
1.	Land and People	9
2.	Precolonial History	16
3.	European Contact, Colonial Rule, and Independence	22
4.	Religion and Culture	28
5.	Daily Life	38
6.	The Arts	44
7.	The Future	57
	Glossary	61
	For Further Reading	62
	Index	63

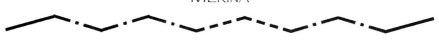

INTRODUCTION

THERE IS EVERY REASON FOR US TO KNOW something about Africa and to understand its past and the way of life of its peoples. Africa is a rich continent that has for centuries provided the world with art, culture, labor, wealth, and natural resources. It has vast mineral deposits, fossil fuels, and commercial crops.

But perhaps most important is the fact that fossil evidence indicates that human beings originated in Africa. The earliest traces of human beings and their tools are almost two million years old. Their descendants have migrated throughout the world. To be human is to be of African descent.

The experiences of the peoples who stayed in Africa are as rich and as diverse as of those who established themselves elsewhere. This series of books describes their environment, their modes of subsistence, their relationships, and their customs and beliefs. The books present the variety of languages, histories, cultures, and religions that are to be found on the African continent. They demonstrate the historical linkages between African peoples and the way contemporary Africa has been affected by European colonial rule.

Africa is large, complex, and diverse. It encompasses an area of more than 11,700,000

Introduction

square miles. The United States, Europe, and India could fit easily into it. The sheer size is an indication of the continent's great variety in geography, terrain, climate, flora, fauna, peoples, languages, and cultures.

Much of contemporary Africa has been shaped by European colonial rule, industrialization, urbanization, and the demands of a world economic system. For more than seventy years, large regions of Africa were ruled by Great Britain, France, Belgium, Portugal, and Spain. African peoples from various ethnic, linguistic, and cultural backgrounds were brought together to form colonial states.

For decades Africans struggled to gain their independence. It was not until after World War II that the colonial territories became independent African states. Today, almost all of Africa is ruled by Africans. Large numbers of Africans live in modern cities. Rural Africa is also being transformed, and yet its people still engage in many of their customs and beliefs.

Contemporary circumstances and natural events have not always been kind to ordinary Africans. Today, however, new popular social movements and technological innovations pose great promise for future development.

George C. Bond, Ph.D., Director
Institute of African Studies
Columbia University, New York

One of the most important customs of the Merina is the reburial ceremonies, called *famadihana*, that they hold for their ancestors. Here a family gathers around the bundle of a recently rewrapped ancestor.

chapter 1
LAND AND PEOPLE

THE MERINA LIVE IN MADAGASCAR, A LONG, narrow island in the Indian Ocean off the southeastern coast of Africa. Madagascar is only 220 miles away from Africa, across the Mozambique channel.

Compared to Africa on a map, the island appears small. However, Madagascar, called Madagasikara (mah-dah-gah-si-KAR-ah) by the Malagasy people, is large. It is almost 1,000 miles long (1,600 kilometers) and approximately 350 miles wide (560 kilometers). It is the fourth largest island in the world, after Greenland, New Guinea, and Borneo.

The shape of Madagascar's western coast suggests that the island was attached to Africa thousands of years ago. After it broke away, Madagascar evolved in isolation. As a result, it is home to many unique plants and animals.

Map of Madagascar showing the region where the Merina population is concentrated (located inside the red border). Close relatives of the Merina are the Betsileo, who live to the south. Their region is inside the green border.

▼ PEOPLE ▼

Scientists believe Madagascar was not populated until 1000 AD. Archaeological evidence suggests that the first inhabitants were of African and Indonesian descent. They probably came in successive migrations by sea, beginning in Indonesia and following the coastline from Southeast Asia to the Middle East and East Africa. The migrations possibly took hundreds of years or more. During these long journeys, the people met and mixed with others along the way.

Malagasy and Western archaeologists continue to study the area. Many unexplored, ancient sites in Madagascar may yet reveal important information about its human past.

Today Madagascar has eighteen official ethnic groups. Most of the different people live along the coast. The Merina (MARE-in-ah) and the Betsileo (bet-sill-AY-oh) live in the center of the island. They are two of the largest ethnic groups and share many cultural features.

▼ LANGUAGE ▼

Madagascar is unusual because it is one of the only African countries to use one language nationwide. The language, called Malagasy, has Indonesian roots. It also includes influences from Bantu (an African language group), Arabic, French, and English. However, Malagasy has

Malagasy Language

The Malagasy language uses an alphabet similar to English, although it has only twenty-one letters—c, q, u, w, and x are not included. It is based upon the Indonesian language, especially in its structure and vocabulary.

Many Malagasy words are easy to recognize. They are frequently long and often repeat sounds. *Mitsangana* is the Malagasy verb "to walk," while *mitsangantsangana* means "to walk around" or "to hang around." Unlike English, Malagasy verbs almost always begin with the letter "m," such as *manadeha* (to go), *mampihomehy* (to make someone laugh), or *mihinana* (to eat).

Despite its Indonesian roots, Malagasy contains elements of other languages, including Bantu, Arabic, English, and French words. While Malagasy education systems existed before the Europeans arrived, English missionaries were the first people to establish Westernized schools in Madagascar, with classrooms, desks, and books. Therefore, words describing school look and sound like English words. For instance, *pensily* means pencil. *Pegy* means page. *Boky* means book. *Sekoly* means school. Other words also suggest English origins. *Gisa* means goose (from the plural "geese"). *Raopilanina* means aeroplane (the British word for airplane). *Tomobilina* means automobile. A *gilasy* is a drinking glass. The months of the year are also based on English—*Janoary, Febroary, Marsa, Avrily, Mey, Jona, Jolay, Aogositra, Septambra, Oktobra, Novambra,* and *Desambra.*

French people introduced things to Madagascar as well. Words describing these things sound and look French. For instance, *ba* in Malagasy means *bas* (knitting), and *seza* comes from the French *chaise* (chair). The French also imported foods, including *paoma* (*pomme* in French means apple in English), *dibera* (*du beurre* means butter in French), and *dité* (*du thé* is French for tea).

many dialects. Neighboring ethnic groups can understand each other fairly easily. But groups who live far apart—people in the extreme north and south for example—may have difficulty communicating because of strong dialect differences.

▼ CLIMATE AND LANDSCAPE ▼

At its northernmost point, Madagascar lies twelve degrees south of the equator. Its temperature is generally much warmer than that of Europe or North America. Madagascar's location below the equator also means that its seasons are reversed. Its cold winter months are June through September, and its hot, rainy months of summer last from December to March.

The geography of Madagascar varies significantly from place to place. For example, the southern and western coasts feature hot and dry desert, and the eastern coast contains a very thick and humid rain forest.

The area where the Merina people live, called Imerina, is in the center of the island. Some people describe this region as a plateau. But it is more accurately called a highland, because it is not flat. It has many hills, valleys, and rocky outcroppings. The temperature is coolest in the central highlands, reaching the freezing point or lower at night. The soil is deep red and is visible

The part of Madagascar where the Merina live is called Imerina. Seen here is a typical view of the hilly environment (top). Rice is grown in the wet valleys (middle) and on the dry slopes (bottom).

where erosion has occurred. It is common to see pine trees, eucalyptus, and *ravinala* palm trees next to one another. The *ravinala*, whose leaves create a flat, upright fan, is called the traveler's tree. It is one of Madagascar's symbols.

▼ CROPS ▼

A striking feature of the landscape is that rice fields seem to fill every available inch of land. The Merina people consume enormous amounts of rice. It is the main staple of their diet, and most people eat at least one heaping plate every meal. To keep up with the high demand, Merina farmers plant up to two rice crops per year, using both wet and dry farming techniques. Large pools of wet rice extend for miles on the valley floors. Hillsides are also covered with rice, although farmers use a dry planting technique to make use of the uneven ground.

Other major crops include manioc (cassava) and corn. Farmers also grow peanuts, squash, tomatoes, onions, apples, sugarcane, mangoes, pineapples, and melons. Madagascar exports cloves and pepper, although its most important exports are vanilla and coffee. Rice is Madagascar's largest crop, but it is not exported. In fact, additional rice must be imported to meet the internal demand.▲

2
PRECOLONIAL HISTORY

▼ THE FIRST PEOPLE ▼

Central Madagascar's earliest inhabitants were the Vazimba. Little is known about them. They may have been people of a different ethnic background—possibly Indonesian, possibly African. They may have lived in the central highlands before the earliest Merina people arrived, and were then absorbed into the Merina culture. On the other hand, the Vazimba may have been the earliest Merina or pre-Merina people—not a separate, preexisting ethnic group. No one knows for sure. But many Malagasy people continue to respect the Vazimba spirits and sacred Vazimba sites that survive today.

▼ MERINA KINGDOMS ▼

The Merina were a powerful, unified people before Europeans began to colonize the region in the late 1800s. Merina society was based on

King Andrianampoinimerina realized that rice was vital to his kingdom. He introduced new growing systems that doubled productivity. Seen here are rice sellers on the outskirts of Antananarivo, Madagascar's capital.

mpanjaka (royalty), and a system of *andriana* (nobles), *hova* (commoners), and *andevo* (slaves). Although slavery does not exist in Madagascar today, slaves in the past were foreign war captives, the poor, and people who were forced into slavery as punishment for serious crimes.

Andrianampoinimerina (c. 1750–1810) was the first Merina king. Before his reign, the Merina were divided into chiefdoms. He unified the small highland chiefdoms into one kingdom, and established his capital in Antananarivo ("city of a thousand"). This city remains the capital of Madagascar today.

> ### Communicating Through Symbols
>
> In the 1700s, the powerful Merina king, Andrianampoinimerina, was expanding his empire. A Betsileo king, named Andriamanalina, lived to the south and refused to submit to Merina authority. Andrianampoinimerina wanted to send Andriamanalina a message showing the Betsileo his mistake in not recognizing the Merina as rightful king.
>
> He took a piece of cloth, cut a hole in its center, and sent it to Andriamanalina. When Andriamanalina saw the cloth, he understood it to represent his small kingdom (the hole) surrounded by other Betsileo kingdoms (the cloth) who had surrendered and sworn allegiance to Andrianampoinimerina. Andriamanalina was isolated.
>
> The Betsileo king did not want to give up. He sent a cane back to the Merina king. When Andrianampoinimerina saw the cane, he knew he was being challenged to measure himself against the Betsileo king. Whoever was larger and therefore more powerful was the rightful ruler. When Andrianampoinimerina held the cane up, he saw that he was taller than Andriamanalina by an inch.
>
> Andriamanalina refused to surrender because of only one inch. He sacrificed an ox and said that if it died quietly, he would go to war. If the ox bellowed, he would submit. The ox bellowed, but still he waited. Andriamanalina finally surrendered to Andrianampoinimerina only after learning that his son was secretly negotiating with the Merina king.
>
> —adapted from Brown 1978:127

Andrianampoinimerina was the first to create rice irrigation systems that allowed a second planting season. He also set up a system of weekly markets, a new administrative structure, new religious practices, and a strong, centrally controlled military. All these systems were essential in organizing and controlling large groups of people under one ruler.

Andrianampoinimerina once said, "Rice and I

King Andrianampoinimerina introduced weekly markets for selling farm products, such as the fruit displayed at this market in Arivonimamo.

are one," showing how essential rice and agriculture were to his ability to expand and control his kingdom. Some believe he told his son, "The ocean is the limit of my rice fields." This statement was meant to challenge his son to expand Merina control to the coast.

Andrianampoinimerina's son Radama I ruled from 1810 to 1828. He extended his control to the ocean, just as his father had wished. He was the first Merina *mpanjaka* to make treaties with European rulers. He was interested in European customs, from dress to military training. He welcomed European missionaries and allowed them to preach, establish schools, and teach their European ways.

Ranavalona I, who ruled from 1828 to 1861, was a powerful queen. She was so powerful and strong-willed that many written accounts call her evil. Indeed, she was often brutal and unpredictable. She alternately allowed religious freedom, then persecuted Malagasy Christians who refused to give up their new faith.

Ranavalona I lived during a difficult, changing time. It was an era of meshing traditional Malagasy life with conflicting new religions and ideas. Before her, Radama I had embraced European ideas. So Ranavalona I was condemned by outsiders when she tried to return to the life of earlier times before Westernization had taken hold. However, she did not invent the severe methods she used. She was simply the last ruler to continue existing traditions.

Queen Ranavalona II ruled from 1868 to 1885. (She came to power following the short reigns of Ranavalona I's son, Radama II, from 1861 to 1863, and Radama II's wife, Rasoherina, from 1863 to 1868.) In 1869, Ranavalona II became the first Malagasy ruler to convert to Christianity. She then ordered the

The Queen's Palace, or Rova, in Antananarivo (above left), was built in the 1600s. Unfortunately, it was destroyed by fire in November 1995.

destruction of the royal *sampy*, the sacred and powerful amulets of the kingdom. Made by religious experts, *sampy* protected the rulers and their kingdoms against misfortune in much the same way that St. Christopher medals are said to protect Catholic travelers.

Ranavalona II's husband, Rainilaiarivony, was Prime Minister. He married three consecutive Merina queens: Rasoherina, Ranavalona II, and Ranavalona III. Ranavalona III was the last Merina ruler. She died in exile after Madagascar became a French colony in 1895. ▲

chapter

3

EUROPEAN CONTACT, COLONIAL RULE, AND INDEPENDENCE

ANCIENT ARAB TRADE NETWORKS EXTENDED across Asia, Africa, and the Middle East. Traders wrote the earliest accounts of an island off Africa's southeast coast. The Venetian explorer Marco Polo first gave Madagascar its name in the 1200s, although he never went there.

Portuguese sailors reached Madagascar in 1500 and named it São Lourenço, or Saint Laurence, because they first saw the island on that saint's feast day. The Portuguese never ventured inland from the coast, and finally left Madagascar in the 1600s. They had decided that the Malagasy people would never convert to Christianity, nor would the island be profitable.

The Dutch, French, and English arrived in the late 1500s and early 1600s. At first, they exchanged goods for fresh supplies. Later, they built forts and sent colonists, but the settlements failed.

Madagascar was an important stop for European ships on their way to and from the Spice Islands in the East. The spice trade was highly competitive and involved large sums of money. Many ships filled with riches crossed the Indian Ocean. Some dealt in the spice trade, others were on pilgrimage to Mecca, and some were owned by rich Middle Eastern moguls. Whatever their cargo, they attracted additional attention—from pirates. Soon Madagascar and its neighboring islands became safe havens for a growing number of pirate ships.

In the 1800s, the English and French renewed their interest in Madagascar. Protestant missionaries from England and Catholic missionaries from France vied for the favor of the Merina royalty. Sometimes, the Merina kings and queens chose the religion of individual missionaries or settlers whose skills most benefitted the Merina. Thus, the Merina profited considerably from competition between the Europeans. In an attempt to gain the favor of Merina royalty, the Europeans established official diplomatic relations, founded schools and missions, and developed industrial and military technology in the region.

▼ MADAGASCAR AS A COLONY ▼

Madagascar was colonized by the French in 1895. Queen Ranavalona III and the Prime

Minister were exiled to Algeria, and a French governing body was established. Many French settlers arrived and were treated as French citizens. The Malagasy people, however, were subject to a separate legal system. Part of this system required the Malagasy to submit to *corvée* (forced labor). This meant that they had to work a certain number of days without pay for the French government each month, while paying extra taxes on other earnings and on each head of cattle they owned. The French thought of the colony as a resource. During World War II, Madagascar supplied people and materials to France's war effort in Europe.

Colonization produced unrest among the Malagasy, particularly during the Rebellion of 1947. Thousands of people died fighting against French colonization. Contributing to the high number of dead and wounded was the fact that the Malagasy people were divided among themselves. Although most Malagasy wanted to end colonial rule, not all Malagasy people supported the rebellion. The resulting revolt resembled a civil war more than a unified fight for independence.

▼ INDEPENDENCE ▼

Madagascar achieved full independence from France on June 26, 1960. Today, most celebration occurs the evening before Independence

On the eve of Independence Day, children carry brightly colored lanterns lit with candles, such as the ones on sale here.

Day. The landscape twinkles with bonfires, and children parade up and down the streets carrying brightly painted paper lanterns of all shapes and sizes, each glowing with a small candle.

The first Malagasy president upon independence was Philibert Tsiranana, who founded the First Republic. The Second Republic was established in 1975 by a naval officer, Didier Ratsiraka. He introduced socialist policies, including nationalizing banks and expelling Western capitalists. Soon the economy suffered, and the people began to protest. Civil unrest finally convinced the president to hold island-

Malagasy National Anthem

Ry tanin-drazanay malala—ô,	Our beloved ancestral land,
Ry Madagasikara soa.	Beautiful Madagascar.
Ny fitiavanao tsy miala,	Our love for you will not die,
Fa ho anao, ho anao, dory tokoa.	To you forever and always.
Tahionao ry Zanahary,	God blesses you,
Ity nosin-drazanay ity.	This ancestral island of ours.
Hiadana sy hafinaritra,	At peace and joy,
Hé sambatra tokoa izahay.	We are truly blessed.

Malagasy schools are based on the French system of education. Students wear uniforms whose colors correspond to their school level. The youngest grades (similar to American elementary school) wear tan, while older grades wear blue. Students begin their school day in assembly, singing the national anthem.

wide elections in an attempt to keep control.

Madagascar's Third Republic began in 1993, when Professor Albert Zafy defeated Ratsiraka in the presidential election. The latest Republic embraces the democratic principles of multiple political parties and a free-market economy. ▲

The Third Republic's first leader was President Albert Zafy. Seen here is a rally celebrating his inauguration in Antananarivo in March 1993.

chapter 4
RELIGION AND CULTURE

MANY DIFFERENT RELIGIONS ARE PRACTICED in Madagascar. Most Merina are Christian, and mainly Catholic or Protestant. But being a Christian does not exclude a person from continuing older Malagasy beliefs concerning the ancestors. The Merina do not believe that it is a contradiction to attend a Christian church and participate in ancestral ceremonies.

In Malagasy culture, marriage combines Christian and indigenous customs. Merina people have three different marriage ceremonies. A couple may perform one, two, or all three, depending on their religious beliefs and financial status. The first marriage is a civil ceremony, performed at the local town hall. The couple and their witnesses sign the marriage certificate, generally before a large audience. Most couples, however, also perform the *vodin-ondry*. *Vodin-ondry* means "sheep rump," the fatty part of the sheep reserved for elders and honored individuals when meat is distributed. In the context of marriage, however, it means "bride-price." This refers to the ceremony when the groom and his family go to the bride's house with their dowry payment. After speeches and a meal, the bride returns home with the groom, bringing the bride goods given by her family. The third marriage ceremony follows the tradition of the bride and groom's church and may closely resemble an American or European wedding.

Another Merina custom involves male circumcision. This ceremony, which is not performed for girls, can also combine Western and Merina practices. Some boys are circumcised in a hospital as babies, with no accompanying Merina ceremony. Other boys are circumcised by a doctor or circumcision specialist at home, in the dark hours before dawn, surrounded by music, dancing, singing, friends, and family. In this case, the operation takes place in a room filled with men, while women and children wait outside, singing, dancing, and spraying sacred water as a blessing. The operation is followed by symbolic battles over sugarcane, gifts from the family to the guests, speeches of thanks, blessings, and a meal.

▼ ANCESTRAL LAND ▼

Family is important to the Merina. Life

Tanin-drazana, ancestral land, is closely connected to the ancestral tomb, and the family house, which is passed down from generation to generation. This home is near Betafo in the Merina countryside.

revolves around one's family. It provides strength and resources, requires many responsibilities, and plays a fundamental role in forming one's identity.

Family ties are strongly linked to the *tanin-drazana*, the land that was occupied by one's ancestors. *Tanin-drazana* is identified with two ancestral homes—a two-storied brick house passed down among the living and, more importantly, the stone tomb, called a *fasana*, of the family's ancestors. The significance of the tomb is so great that upon meeting someone new, a Merina does not ask, "Where are you from?" but instead, "Where is your family tomb?"

▼ THE ANCESTORS ▼

In Madagascar, as in many parts of the world, life is thought of as a progression. For Merina people, life does not begin at birth and end at death, but continues into another, parallel world of the ancestors.

Ancestors play an important role in a person's life. They can affect the lives of their descendants, both positively and negatively. Therefore, the living do not make important decisions without consulting the ancestors. A student who is about to take an important exam or choose a major, a woman thinking about starting a business, or a man deciding whether to take a new job and move to a new town, will each consult their ancestors before making their decisions.

Elderly people, however, are believed to have the closest contact with the ancestors. Elders sit on the threshold between the worlds of the living and the dead. Their position allows them to have greater access to, and therefore influence over, the ancestors' world and the ancestors themselves.

The ancestors communicate with the living in a number of ways. They can alter the lives of their descendants—causing misfortune if they are dissatisfied, or good fortune if they are happy. They may also talk directly to their descendants in dreams. Sometimes, however, messages are unclear. At other times someone may want to ask a specific question of the ancestors. In such instances, divination can clarify or explain the matter.

Divination is a system of understanding and communicating with the less-visible ancestral and spiritual worlds. Diviners, who may be either male or female, are experts in interpreting the divination system and the messages within it.

Different kinds of divination exist. Generally, a diviner consults the cardinal points (north, south, east, west) and the calendar and number systems, and uses color symbolism. Each system is so complex that only a specialist diviner can interpret the signs correctly. For example, strict rules govern what events should occur and when. Each day of the week is associated with a particular destiny, a set of characteristics, and a color or colors.

The living communicate with their ancestors through actions. Caring for the ancestors and following tradition shows the ancestors that they are remembered and respected. The Merina believe that life in the ancestors' parallel world continues much as it did while the dead were alive. They continue to work, eat, sleep, and interact. A farmer still works in his fields, a weaver still weaves, and a business owner still runs a business. Ancestors also continue to have needs similar to those of the living. They must have clothes (a burial shroud) and a home (a tomb) kept in good condition to stay happy and warm. A family's relationship with its ancestors is reciprocal. As long as a family cares for its ancestors' needs, the ancestors will care for the family in return.

▼ ANCESTRAL CULTURE AND ▼ THE *FAMADIHANA*

The Merina and neighboring Betsileo have funeral customs that are specific to Madagascar's central highlands. When a person dies, a funeral is held immediately. Then, one to twenty years after the initial funeral, Merina and Betsileo people begin performing reburials, called *famadihana*. These recurring ceremonies last one to four days, during which the deceased's family and community gather for speeches, music, dancing, and feasting. Family and community ties are strengthened, as are those with the ancestors. In fact, the motive for performing a *famadihana* is to return the deceased to the *tanin-drazana* (ancestral land) for inclusion in the family tomb, and especially to give the ancestors new burial shrouds.

Ancestors are wrapped in *lambamena* (burial shrouds) during the initial funeral and each reburial ceremony. Shrouds are large cotton or silk cloths whose number and size depend on the social and financial status of the deceased person and his or her family. Although

Red is associated with royalty, power, and respect. Here, a *lambamena* vendor holds up a shroud composed largely of red threads.

lambamena means "red cloth," the shroud does not have to be red. This name may refer to the cloth's traditional color, or to red's symbolic association with royalty and power, and, therefore, with respect.

The timing of the periodic reburials is based upon family or regional tradition and the instructions of a diviner. The ancestors may also initiate a *famadihana* by communicating to their descendants that they are unhappy. They may do this by causing misfortune. They also may appear in dreams to say they feel neglected or that they are "cold" due to the poor condition of their tombs or shrouds.

The Merina do not allow their ancestors' shrouds to disintegrate. Allowing one's ancestors to dress in rags, and thus experience cold, is disrespectful. To bury someone without a

During reburial ceremonies, the remains of ancestors who have died far from home are carried to the *fasana*, the family tomb. This *famadihana* ceremony was held near Antananarivo in 1992.

lambamena tells the community that the deceased is not someone of worth, and not entitled to respect. Such a person is compared to a dog, which is not given a shroud when buried. Therefore, burial shrouds visually separate humans from animals, and Malagasy people from non-Malagasy.

While death and funerals are moments of great sadness, reburials are surrounded by celebration. The deceased is finally joining the ancestors in the family tomb. There he or she will no longer be lonely or cold, and the living will be able to care for his or her needs.

Famadihana allow the living to experience and work through their grief, and to overcome it. Mourners follow specific rules to care for their ancestors. By doing so, they know they are

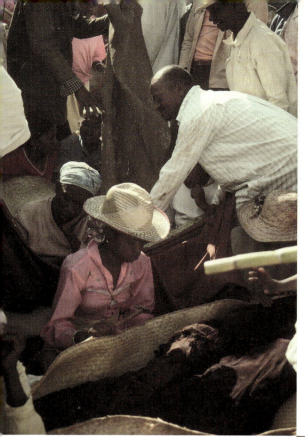

During reburials, relatives talk to their ancestors and give them gifts.

At a ceremony near Ambatofotsy in 1993 (right), some ancestors are placed on *tsihy* mats for rewrapping, while other family members dance with other ancestors on their shoulders.

making their ancestral family happy. *Famadihana* also allow the living to continue interacting with the dead by talking, comforting, questioning, and touching them. Throughout the ceremony, the living publicly communicate with relatives who have died, rather than deal with their emotions privately. The living find comfort knowing exactly where each person will be buried, surrounded by family, for eternity. Therefore, reburial ceremonies are happy events accompanied by much celebration.

The ancestors' possessions, especially those that have crossed from the world of the living into that of the dead, are highly valued. Burial shrouds, beads from shrouds, and matting are thought to convey the ancestors' blessings. For example, a woman carrying a new shroud for use in a reburial ceremony may loop the cloth over one shoulder and around her opposite hip. She may also dance with it draped over both shoulders, ends grasped in her raised hands, while waiting for the tomb door to open and the ancestors to be carried out. Through physical contact with the ancestors' possessions, the woman hopes to receive the ancestors' blessings. ▲

chapter 5
DAILY LIFE

▼ OCCUPATIONS ▼

Merina people enjoy a high degree of equality between genders. Men and women can become doctors, lawyers, business owners, schoolteachers, and politicians. Before colonization, kings and queens ruled the Merina kingdom. Yet, some differences do exist between the roles of men and women. Men, for example, often have jobs requiring strength or providing protection, and women are generally caregivers. However, greater significance is placed on whether a person lives in the city or country, because of differences in lifestyle, occupation, and wealth.

City people have urban jobs. They are businesspeople, government employees, bankers, taxi drivers, telephone operators, and teachers. Similar jobs are found in the country, but on a smaller scale, or changed to fit country life. For

Antananarivo is a busy city. Buses and taxis transport many people to work.

example, country versions of taxis are *taxi brousses*, "bush taxis" that cross the countryside rather than driving across town.

Most Merina are farmers. Everyone grows at least some rice, and many grow fruits and vegetables. Farmers also raise cattle, called *omby*. *Omby* have long, curved horns, and are zebu cattle, a kind that has a large hump on their shoulders. People living in the country often prefer to safeguard their wealth by investing in cattle rather than in a bank. A family with many *omby* is a wealthy family.

Individuals and families are often involved in multiple occupations. For example, a farmer may also sell produce in the market, run another

Merina

How much does it cost?

It was Wednesday—market day in town. "Ravo," her mom called, "I want to make *ravintoto* for dinner. Please go to the market for me. Here is some money." "Yes, *Neny*," Ravo answered. She liked going to the market for her mom when she made the heavy sauce of pounded manioc leaves and pork called *ravintoto*. It was her favorite.

Ravo's mom gave her some brightly colored bills. She handed her a small, brown 500 *fmg* with a picture of a little boy holding a fish he'd just caught, a purple 1,000 *fmg* with the famous flute player on it, and a handful of coins. She also gave Ravo a 2,500 *fmg* with a bird, tortoise, lemur, and butterfly drawn on it in a rainbow of colors, and a bigger, blue 5,000 *fmg* with a woman carrying a baby on her back. Ravo really liked the big, green 10,000 *fmg* with a little girl holding rice stalks that she had just helped to harvest. But Ravo knew she would not need that much money for just a few things.

Ravo put the money in her pocket, took down a red and turquoise raffia basket, and walked down the road to the marketplace. She went first to Bebe, the onion woman, and bought a small pile of four white onions. Bebe asked Ravo for 70 *ariary*. Ravo had to think. Each piece of Malagasy money can be counted in two different ways. One way to count it is by Malagasy *ariary* (a); the other way of counting, began during the time of French colonization, is by *franc Malgache* (fmg). One *ariary* equals five *francs Malgache*. Bebe had asked for 350 *fmg*. That was too much! Ravo bargained with the woman. She knew a small pile of onions should cost 300 *fmg*. "I can only pay 50 *ariary*," Ravo said, beginning to bargain with a low price. "Oh, my. That is too small. How can I stay in business if I collect that little amount?" Bebe asked. Ravo liked Bebe, because she bargained with Ravo like an adult. Bebe means grandmother, and everyone called her that out of respect because she was very old. Finally, Ravo and Bebe agreed on a price—60 *ariary*. Ravo handed Bebe her brown 500 *fmg* note, and Bebe gave her back two coins of 20a each. Ravo counted the change—200 *fmg* was correct.

"*Misaotra betsaka*, Bebe. Thank you very much," Ravo said, as she put the onions in her basket. Bebe gave her a small onion as a "gift" because the transaction went well and they were both happy. Ravo smiled and went to see the woman selling tomatoes for 62a (310 fmg), and manioc for 49a (245 *fmg*). After spending 200a (1000 *fmg*) at the butcher's, Ravo looked for Rakoto, the man selling rice. Malagasy people eat a lot of rice every day. The Malagasy even have a saying, "You haven't eaten a meal if you haven't eaten rice." Ravo bought her rice last because that much rice is heavy to carry. She bought 20 *kapoaka* (measured in a can) from Rakoto, who counted aloud as he poured each *kapoaka* of rice into her basket. Ravo paid 36a for each can (3600 *fmg*), and walked home to help her mom make *ravintoto*. She was hungry.

small business, use the family car as a taxi, and weave and sell baskets.

▼ FAMILY LIFE ▼

Merina families may include many generations. Often, especially in the country, extended families live together or near one another. This is partially due to the importance of one's ancestral land. People want to return to their land and family in times of crisis and in old age. Large families are also a source of wealth. Having many family members means there are many

The official currency of Madagascar, the *franc Malagache* (*fmg*), was introduced during French colonization. Before this, Malagasy also counted money in *ariary* (a). Today, prices can be quoted in either *fmg* or *ariary*.

Family life is very important to the Merina. Particularly in rural areas, several generations of one family usually live together in the same house.

hands to work in the fields. Large families take care of each other. They provide a form of social security in a poor country where pensions are rare. Young family members care for elders, and the wealthy help less fortunate relations by taking them in.

Names, especially last names, are often chosen from relatives. They are not necessarily shared between husband and wife, or among brother and sister. Children frequently receive the name of a grandparent, forming a special, cross-generational tie. Special ties also develop between siblings or cousins, who are often considered "brothers" or "sisters." Merina children are given more responsibility at a younger age than children in many Western societies. Children often care for younger brothers and sisters. Five-year-olds may carry two- and three-year-old children, who are secured to their backs with cloth, wherever they go.

▼ CHORES ▼

Days are filled with work. Children fetch water at the local river or water hole. Laundry is washed at the river's edge on large, flat stones. Women pound rice with a mortar and pestle to remove the husk from the white grain. They cook over a wood fire. Breakfast is often *vary sosoa* (rice porridge). Lunch is the biggest meal of the day. Usually, rice with sauce is served, accompanied by *rano vola* ("gold water"), water heated in the pot of leftover rice. Dinner is frequently reheated leftovers from lunch. Electricity is rarely available in the countryside, so perishable foods cannot be refrigerated—someone must go to the market every day.

At the end of the day, families may tell stories, play games, sing, and enjoy many of the same kinds of recreation found throughout the world. Music is very popular, as are dancing and videos. City people have ready access to such entertainment. It is sometimes available in the countryside as well, thanks to gas-powered generators and car batteries capable of running electronics.▲

chapter 6
THE ARTS

MANY PEOPLE LIVING IN HIGHLAND Madagascar are poor. They often cannot afford the expensive imports that are common in many other countries. Yet this is an economic poverty, not a poverty of culture. Madagascar's material culture—its arts—is a rich and important part of every Merina person's life.

▼ LOOM WEAVING ▼

Weaving is an important artistic and economic activity in Imerina. Weavers are usually women, although men sometimes weave as well. There are two main types of weaving: loom weaving of cloth, and hand weaving of raffia baskets, mats, and hats. Looms can be operated by machine or by hand. Most Merina weavers operate small, wooden hand looms in their homes. *Lambamena* burial shrouds, tablecloths, and bedspreads are loom-woven.

Another cloth that is loom-woven is the *lamba*, a shawl worn by Merina men and women. Men's *lamba* are large, while women's are usually smaller. *Lamba* are versatile. Men generally wrap them around their shoulders or drape them over one shoulder. *Lamba* are also useful when traveling. They serve as ground covers and as blankets at night.

A woman may wrap her *lamba* around her torso to carry a baby or small child on her back (something that men and children sometimes do also). She may roll the cloth into a small coil on her head to balance and soften heavy loads, such as water, firewood, or boxes that she carries on her head. *Lamba* are also useful as apron-like coverings to protect one's clothes while working. This is especially important in a poor country, where most people buy new clothes infrequently. Finally, long, thin *lamba* are important on special occasions. Even if dressed poorly, a woman can wear this formal *lamba* and know she is dressed in a traditional and appropriate way.

▼ HAND WEAVING ▼

Raffia is woven by hand to make mats (*tsihy*), baskets (*sobiky*), and hats (*satroka*).

Tsihy are large, rectangular mats used as floor coverings. They provide a portable, clean place to sit during trips—benches or other seats are rarely available out-of-doors. During *famadihana* (reburials), ancestors are carried from the tomb in newly woven *tsihy* mats and laid upon them while being re-enshrouded. Mats create a special, temporary environment that is protective and spiritually powerful. They contain the ancestors' remains and shield them from possible contamination until they are once again wrapped in new burial shrouds.

Baskets, or *sobiky*, are made in all sizes. They generally resemble *tsihy* mats in the way they are decorated and designed. They are made from individual, cream-colored reeds that are dyed red, blue, and green. The pieces are then interwoven to create simple or brilliant geometric designs.

Hats offer men, women, and children protection from the sun. *Satroka* also have recognizable regional styles based on coloring, size, and shape. They may be plain or have geometric designs similar to mats and baskets. Some have large and wide brims, while other brims are small, turned up, or absent altogether. A hat's crown may be round, square, pointed, or oval. Although most hats are woven raffia, others are long, braided raffia strips that are coiled and sewn into place.

▼ ORAL ARTS ▼

Speaking eloquently in Madagascar is an important and highly respected skill. Daily speech is

Weaving is an important art form. This raffia mat has a proverb that says, "No one has enough for themselves, so blessed are those who help others."

sprinkled with proverbs, especially among elders. Proverbs allow someone to make a point while avoiding confrontation or embarrassment. Proverbs also help the speaker convey his or her message eloquently.

Ceremonial speech, called *kabary*, is a formal, stylized speech used on all important occasions. Orators who perform beautiful *kabary* are recognized as highly talented. A good *kabary* is discussed, critiqued, and appreciated long after it is over.

Singing is another important oral art form. *Hira gasy* are musical competitions between two troupes lasting two days. They may be performed as part of a *famadihana* ceremony. Troupes write and practice new songs each year during the quiet summer months until they have a polished act for the winter ceremony season. *Hira gasy* performances thoughtfully ask moral, political, and social questions and raise important issues. Songs address current subjects—

Ohabolana (Proverbs)

Ny vary tsy fotsy tsy an-daona.
Rice is white only if it is pounded in the mortar.
(You must work for what you want.)

Isika maty iray fasana, velona iray trano.
One tomb in death, one house in life.
(Shows the importance of family and togetherness.)

Aza mitoto vary an-trano fohy loha.
Do not pound rice in a house with a low roof.
(Do not do something without first thinking it through.)

Vorombe kely atody.
A large bird has a little egg.
(A big person comes from small beginnings.)

Tanora ratsy fihary, antitra vao ratsy laoka.
A youth works poorly, an elder has little to eat.
(Waste in youth and there will be nothing in old age.)

political leadership, miscommunication between generations, proper moral behavior, or changing Malagasy culture. The audience critiques the skills of the singers, musicians, and acrobats, as well as the relevance of the subject matter. Listeners memorize the best songs, and sing along during subsequent performances.

Hira gasy competitions during *famadihana* include another performance, called *zana-drazana* ("children of the ancestors"). During the *zana-drazana*, family members parade and dance together, wearing matching outfits, such as shirts, dresses, or suits of similar fabric. While parading, the ancestors' family gives extra money to the *hira gasy* singing troupes, the tomb

Hira gasy musical troupes compete in the winter.

builders, and the family heads in recognition and appreciation of a job well done.

▼ MUSIC ▼

Hira gasy musical troupes sing and perform to various instruments, mainly the violin, trumpet, and drum. Other musicians play during *famadihana* reburial ceremonies, and may incorporate some combination of drums, violin, trumpet, accordion, ukelele, and flute. Some bands include many musicians playing the same instrument.

Modern pop music blends the sounds of traditional Malagasy instruments with those more recently introduced to the island. For example, a *valiha* (a type of bamboo harp) may be played with an accordion, electric guitar, and drum set. Malagasy bands, such as Tarika, Rossy, Dama, or Rakoto Frah, are earning widespread reputations outside of Madagascar, and now tour Europe and the United States.

Where there is music, there is also dancing. In the city, and especially at discotheques (night clubs or dance bars), American swing dancing, called by the French term *"le rock,"* is very popular. Traditional Merina dancing, however, is common during ceremonial events and in the countryside. Line dancing is performed either with or without partners. Other styles allow individual dancing in a center circle. Women generally dance slowly and gracefully. Some dance with their elbows out and hands upstretched, or with their hands on their hips, thrusting alternate shoulders forward and back. Men, on the other hand, have a more aggressive style, dramatically stomping their feet to the music.

▼ ARCHITECTURE ▼

The highland countryside is dotted by two types of architecture; one houses the living and the other houses the dead. Homes for the living are usually two-storied brick and wood structures that blend into the landscape. Tombs are constructed of stone and can be seen for miles.

Homes vary depending on location and the family's wealth. City people may live in apartments. Wealthy people may live in large, fancy mansions. Most people, however, live in rectangular, two-story, brick houses with thatched roofs. Bricks are made from red clay that is pressed into rectangular wooden molds. The wet clay bricks are then stacked into a high, square pile, whose center is filled with straw. The center

Malagasy homes vary according to location and the family's wealth. Many city families live in apartment buildings (above). Most people in the Imerina region live in two-story brick homes, often with verandas (below).

is then lit, and the brick pile becomes its own oven, containing heat and baking itself.

Houses often have the same floor plan. The door is usually located in the center of one long wall, with a window on one or both sides of it. Each floor is split into two large rooms, frequently separated by a staircase. The second floor usually has a large wooden balcony. If not, the house is built with a preexisting door and floor supports so that one may be added later. Often, different generations occupy different rooms or floors.

Merina tombs, called *fasana*, vary in size and form. The basic layout, however, is a square stone vault. Three of the walls have vertical shelves on which the ancestors rest. Older tombs are often completely underground and capped by a stepped pyramid structure of earth and stone. Newer tombs, built within the last few generations, are angular structures that are partially underground. Their exteriors resemble stone cubes, although they may include elaborate, decorative superstructures, stairways, archways, or sculptures.

Tomb decoration varies depending on the region, family, and tomb builder. Decorations may take the forms of sculptures, carvings, or paintings, and may appear on the outside of the tomb or remain hidden inside. Designs often include floral or geometric patterns, or images

Merina tombs, called *fasana*, have many different forms. This example, built partially underground, has a gated area in the front and is decorated with Christian crosses.

inspired by events in the tomb owner's life. They may also illustrate a family's important possessions, occupations, religion, or wartime experiences. Other decoration creates or emphasizes a tomb's architectural elements, as when the mortar holding the stone blocks together is brightly painted, or when a flat stone portal is carved to resemble an actual panelled door.

Sometimes it is impossible to include all deceased family members in the ancestral tomb. They could live in another country or die far from home, possibly while fighting a war overseas. If this is the case, the family will construct a memorial monument to that person.

Vatolahy ("male stones") and *tsangam-bato* ("standing stones") are large, flat, stone slabs raised in honor of a deceased person or an event. Found throughout Imerina, *vatolahy* are

Vatolahy, literally "male stones," are memorial stones found erected in Imerina country.

plain stones showing the family's love and respect through the act of being purchased and raised. This is not a simple feat, since they can reach a height of eighteen feet or more. Decorated *tsangam-bato* include painted, engraved, or sculpted designs similar to tombs, and may include words. The words usually acknowledge the honor and character of the deceased, and the love of the family who erected it.

Another striking form of Merina architecture exists in old towns and villages. Deep ditches are still visible from previously fortified villages that had been surrounded by high stone walls and dry moats. While fortification is no longer necessary, the ditches remain. So do the ancient gateways that were part of these protective barriers. In the past, gateways were secured at night by rolling giant stone wheels across the openings.

Many items woven in raffia by Merina people, such as the baskets, hats, and stools seen here, are popular with tourists today.

▼ TOURIST ARTS ▼

Merina people are very much aware of the world outside of Madagascar. They create and sell objects and art that tourists and businesspeople buy as souvenirs. Some objects are statements about what it means to be Malagasy, or what artists think foreigners expect it to mean.

Vendors in Antananarivo's open-air art markets sell many different items, including model cars made from tin cans; toy lemurs (small mammals that are related to monkeys and live almost exclusively in Madagascar); silk paintings; games; woven goods; fossilized eggs of the giant, extinct, aepyornis bird; and jewelry of cattle horn, tortoise shell, gold, silver, and precious or semiprecious stone. Also available are decorative maps of Madagascar made of semiprecious stone, or highlighted with miniature lemurs, musical instruments, or other images that are "typically" Malagasy.▲

chapter 7
THE FUTURE

POVERTY IS ONE OF THE GREATEST problems facing Madagascar today. As one of the poorest nations in the world, Madagascar has little money and limited resources.

Most Malagasy are very hardworking, often operating several businesses at the same time. Members of a single family, for example, may farm, hire themselves out as field hands, weave, run a small store, work in an office, and sell goods at the weekly market. Families lucky enough to own a car would not miss the opportunity to run a taxi service or carry freight for money. Yet even working this hard, it is difficult to break free of the poverty common to so many Third World countries. Madagascar's great economic hardships have resulted from colonialism, national debt, and falling international prices for its exports.

One problem that has attracted the attention

of Malagasy and foreigners alike is the practice of slash and burn agriculture, called *tanety*. This occurs when large areas of the highland are burned periodically to clear the tall, dry grass and brush for farming or to stimulate new growth for grazing cattle.

Although the highlands were never completely forested, *tanety* has diminished what growth exists. This increases the problem of erosion, resulting in large gullies that continually erode the hillsides, washing away the fertile topsoil. Gullies grow larger and deeper with every rainy season. The pop musician Rossy has a hit song addressing the problem of *tanety*. The chorus repeats one word, "*aoka*," meaning "stop, enough already."

Another problem facing

Poverty is one of the challenges facing Madagascar today. Although starvation is not as great a problem in Madagascar as in other countries, Madagascar's poverty often results in malnutrition. Many poor families eat a lot of rice but very little meat or vegetables. This rural woman pounds rice in a mortar.

The Future

Madagascar today concerns protecting its indigenous and endangered plants and animals. These flora and fauna exist nowhere else. Reserves have been established to protect and study them. However, it is difficult to balance the needs of the endangered plants and animals with those of the people, who depend on them as sources of food. No easy solutions exist. But many people worldwide are working to protect the environment while not depriving the Malagasy people of the resources they need to survive.

Culture continually changes and evolves. However, some Malagasy believe that an important element of Merina culture, the *famadihana* reburial ceremony, is also endangered. According to Merina belief, a person's present and future well-being depends on one's continued good relationship with the ancestors. This relationship depends on successful *famadihana*.

However, some Malagasy are eliminating the indigenous reburial as they adopt and adapt customs and traditions from other cultures. Others, especially poor families, cannot afford to continue performing the expensive ceremony. It is a difficult moral problem for many Merina. If the *famadihana* is not performed due to lack of resources, the ancestors will be unhappy and will withhold good fortune. Yet, spending money beyond a family's means causes further impoverishment that is increasingly difficult to overcome.

Currently, upper-class urban families and less wealthy rural families continue to perform *famadihana*. Reburial practices are undergoing changes that are making it easier for Merina to continue this important tradition without such expense. However, the changes, such as replacing the burial shroud's expensive silk with cheaper materials, are causing conflict and tension over the interpretation of "tradition."

In Madagascar and other developing countries, the potential exists for conflict between Westernization and tradition. Many Merina have no problem living a combined Westernized-Malagasy life. They can work five days a week in a corporate office, use imported Western technology, drive a car, wear Westernized clothing, attend Western churches, and still retain traditional Malagasy values. Other Merina, however, feel a conflict in continuing their local customs, such as reburials, divination, and circumcision.

Some Merina point out that traditions continually grow, change, and evolve as conflicts that arise are worked through and resolved. Customs have always evolved and always will, as long as people grow, change, think, and create. Change is what keeps a tradition alive.▲

Glossary

corvée Forced labor.
divination A system of communicating with the spirit world.
famadihana Reburial ceremonies.
fasana Ancestral tomb.
hira gasy Singing competition often performed during reburials.
Imerina The Merina land or region.
indigenous Something originating locally, as opposed to being imported from a foreign land or culture.
lamba A shawl.
Lambamena A burial shroud.
Malagasy The people living on Madagascar, and the language spoken there.
mpanjaka A ruler, king or queen.
omby Cattle.
outcropping The part of a rock formation that appears at the surface of the ground.
raffia Palm reeds.
tanety A system of clearing land.
tanin-drazana Ancestral land.
troupes A group of travelling performers.
tsangam-bato "Standing stone," raised in honor of an event or deceased person.
vodin-ondry Part of a marriage ceremony.

For Further Reading

Bradt, Hillary. *Guide to Madagascar*. 3rd ed. Chalfont St. Peter, England: Bradt, 1992.

Brown, Mervyn. *Madagascar Rediscovered: A History from Early Times to Independence*. London: Damien Tunnacliffe, 1978.

Covell, Maureen. *Historical Dictionary of Madagascar*. Lanham, MD: Scarecrow Press, 1995.

Kent, Raymond. *Early Kingdoms in Madagascar 1500–1700*. New York: Holt, Rinehart and Winston, 1970.

Mack, John. *Madagascar: Island of the Ancestors*. London: British Museum Publications, 1986.

———. *Malagasy Textiles*. United Kingdom: Shire Publications, 1989.

CHALLENGING READING

Bloch, Maurice. *Placing the Dead: Tombs, Ancestral Villages, and Kinship Organization in Madagascar*. Prospect Heights, IL: Waveland Press, 1994.

Kottak, Conrad, et al., eds. *Madagascar: Society and History*. Durham, NC: Carolina Academic Press, 1986.

Ruud, Jorgen. *Taboo: A Study of Malagasy Customs and Beliefs*. Oslo, Norway: Oslo Press, 1960.

Index

A
ancestors, 28, 30, 31–37, 59
andevo (slaves), 17
andriana (nobles), 17
Andrianampoinimerina, King, 17–19
Antananarivo, 17, 56
architecture, 50–54
ariary (money), 40, 41

B
Betsileo, 11, 33

C
Christianity, 20, 28
circumcision, ceremony of, 29, 60
colonization, 22, 23–24, 57
corvée (forced labor), 24
customs, Merina, 28–29, 33–37, 59–60

D
dancing, 43, 49–50
divination, 32, 34, 60

E
elders, 31, 42
environmental concerns, 58–59
exports, 15, 57

F
famadihana (reburial), 33–37, 45–46, 47, 48, 49, 59–60
farming, 39, 57–58
fasana (tomb), 30, 32–33, 50, 52–53
First Republic, 25
franc Malgache (money), 40, 41

H
hira gasy, (singing competition), 47–49

homes, 30, 50–52
hova (commoners), 17

I
Imerina, 13–15, 44, 53
Indian Ocean, 9, 23
Indonesia, 11, 16

K
kabary (ceremonial speech), 47

L
lamba (shawl), 45
lambamena (burial shroud), 32, 33–35, 37, 44

M
Madagascar, 31, 44, 46, 49, 56, 57, 60
    French colonization of, 21, 23–24
    geography, 9, 13–15
    history, 11, 16–21, 22–23
    independence, 24–26
Madagasikara, 9
Malagasy language, 11–13
manioc, 15
marriage, 28–29
missionaries, 23
mpanjaka (royalty), 17, 20, 23

O
occupations, Merina, 38–41
omby (cattle), 39

P
pirates, 23
Polo, Marco, 22
poverty, 44, 57, 58, 59–60
proverbs, 47, 48

R

Radama I, King, 19–20
raffia, 44, 45
Rainilainriovony, Prime Minister, 21
Ranavalona I, Queen, 20
Ranavalona II, Queen, 20–21
Ranavalona III, Queen, 21, 23
Ratsiraka, 25–26
Rebellion of 1947, 24
recreation, 43
religion, 18, 20, 21, 23, 28–29
rice, 15, 17, 18–19, 39, 43

S

sampy (amulets), 21
São Lourenço (Saint Laurence), 22
satroka (hats), 45, 46
Second Republic, 25
singing, 47–49
sobiky (baskets), 45, 46
speech, 46–47

T

tanety, 58
tanin-drazana (ancestral land), 30, 33, 41
taxi-brousses (bush taxis), 39
Third Republic, 26
tourism, 56
trade, 22, 23
tradition, 32, 60
traveler's tree, 15
tsangam-bato (standing stones), 53–54
tsihy (mats), 45–46
Tsiranana, Philibert, 25

V

vatolahy (male stones), 53–54
Vazimba, 16
vodin-ondry (bride-price), 29

W

weaving, 57
  hand, 44, 45–46
  loom, 44–45
World War II, 24

Z

Zafy, President Albert, 26
zana-drazana (children of the ancestors), 48–49

ABOUT THE AUTHOR:
Currently Professor of non-Western art at Bowling Green State University, Rebecca L. Green earned her B.A. at the University of California Santa Barbara and her M.A. and Ph.D. at Indiana University. Based on almost two years of fieldwork, her dissertation explores ceremony and art among the Merina and Betsileo peoples. She has participated in several national conferences, including the African Studies Association and the Textile Society of America, and has worked at the Indianapolis Museum of Art.

CONSULTING EDITOR: Gary N. van Wyk, Ph.D.

PHOTO CREDITS: All photographs by Rebecca L. Green, Ph.D.

LAYOUT AND DESIGN: Kim Sonsky